WHY don't FISH DROWN?

& other vital questions about the animal kingdom

WHY don't FISH DROWN?

& other vital questions about the animal kingdom

Written by **Anna Claybourne**

With original illustrations by **Claire Goble**

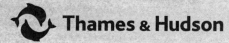 Thames & Hudson

CONTENTS

WHAT is an ANIMAL, ANYWAY?

We all know an animal when we see one. But what makes animals different from vegetables – plants, that is – and other things like rocks and minerals?

Animals and plants are all living things. They can move, grow, and sense their surroundings. But unlike plants, which grow using sunlight, animals eat food – either plants, or other animals. Animals also move around, by running, flying, swimming or slithering, while plants stay in one place.

For thousands of years, people have looked at the animals around them, and asked all kinds of questions about them. Why can't we fly like birds? Why don't animals have to brush their teeth? When animals bark, sing or moo, are they talking to each other? To find out the answers, read on!

Have animals always been here?

Animals have lived on our planet for a LOT longer than humans have. They first appeared on Earth over 500 million years ago. Scientists think the earliest animals were creepy-crawly, worm-like or bug-like creatures that lived in the sea. Gradually, they developed into the millions of different animals we see around us today.

What a Burgess Shale fossil would have looked like when it was alive

What types of animals are there?

Animals can be divided up into two main types, or groups. Invertebrates are animals that don't have a backbone – such as insects and spiders, slugs, octopuses and jellyfish. Vertebrates do have a backbone, and usually a skeleton too. They include five main animal types: fish, reptiles (such as snakes and crocodiles), amphibians (such as frogs and toads), birds and mammals.

A group of frogs, artist unknown, c. 1851

Are humans animals too?

Absolutely. Humans have backbones, so we belong to the vertebrate group of animals. We are mammals, just like many of the animals we feel most familiar with: dogs and cats, horses, dolphins and elephants. Our closest relatives, though, are the apes: animals like gorillas, orangutans and chimpanzees. Take a look at their faces, hands and feet, and you'll see just how similar we are!

A family of bonobo monkeys

Who PICKS THE NAMES for ANIMALS?

If you discover a new type of animal, YOU get to name it!

That doesn't just mean you get to call it Tigger, Fluffykins or Bob (although you can do that too!). It means you get to give that type, or species, of animal its **scientific Latin name**. This means that whichever language they speak themselves, animal scientists around the world can always use the **Latin name** to be sure which animal they're talking about.

Each species gets its own **unique**

HOMO SAPIENS

Beyonce

LOOK
at this fly's
fabulous,
golden behind

name, made up of two words. The names are written in Latin, an **old language** that is no longer spoken.

Sometimes, animals are named after the **person who discovered them**, or after someone famous. For example, in 2011, a species of fly was named Scaptia beyonceae after the singer Beyoncé.

A Scaptia beyonceae fly

Animals can be sorted into family groups that are closely related. Like the cat family, for example. Tigers, lions, cheetahs and pet cats are all in this family, and although they come in many sizes, they're all similar.

But, did you know that ALL animals are actually related? Chimps and gorillas may be your closest cousins, but cats, crocodiles, ostriches, lobsters and woodlice are your relatives too. Scientists believe we all evolved, or developed over time, from the first simple life form – so we're all basically one family.

An ermine tea party, Plocquet and Guttart, 1851

ONE BIG HAPPY FAMILY!

WHAT'S YOUR NAME?

Latin names may sound like gobbledygook, but they are often chosen to describe the animal's features. The humpback whale's scientific name is *Megaptera novaeangliae*, which literally means 'Big wings from New England'. Its 'wings' are its enormous flippers, which it uses to glide through the sea as if it is flying. And what about *Ailuropoda melanoleuca*? That means 'Cat-footed, black and white'. It's the giant panda. And as for *Homo sapiens*, that's you! It means 'human who knows' or 'smart human'.

A giant panda sticking its tongue out

THE GREAT UNKNOWN

We already know about thousands of animal species, but scientists still find new ones every day. They are usually pretty small ones, like beetles and worms – although sometimes they'll find something bigger, like the Kabomani tapir, discovered in 2013.

Before announcing their discovery, scientists have to study their new animal carefully to be sure it really is previously unknown.

The newly discovered Kabomani tapir

Where did ANIMALS COME FROM?

If life started off as one type of living thing, why do we have millions now?

It's because of **evolution** – the way living species gradually **change over time**. As animals move around, they spread out and start living in different places, or habitats. All animals are slightly different, even in the same species. The ones that are the best at living in a particular habitat are the ones that survive longest there. They have more babies, and pass on their features to them. So, slowly, species become **more suited to their habitats**, and more different from each other.

CAN ➤➤
you spot
the lizard?

That's why you get fast, torpedo-shaped sharks in the sea, with fins and gills — while in the jungle, you'll find monkeys with hands and prehensile tails for grabbing branches. And, although **it happens gradually**, animals are still evolving and changing today. For example, scientists have found that some types of rats are evolving to become immune to rat poison.

A camouflaged lizard

Why don't humans have tails?
Go to page 16

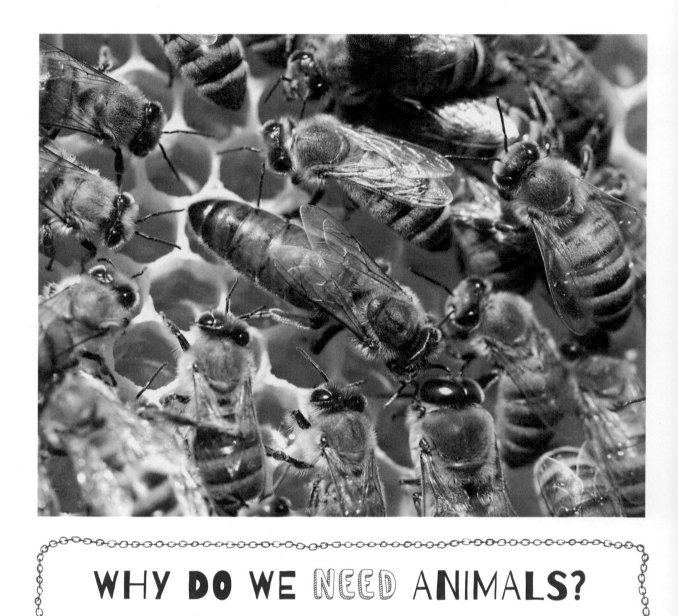

WHY **DO** WE NEED ANIMALS?

The world and its plants, animals, humans and other living things make up an ecosystem. This means they work together as a whole. Each living thing provides food for others, and helps to balance the whole system.

Insects, for example, spread pollen between plants, which helps the plants to make seeds and fruit. Worms burrow through the soil, which breaks it up and makes it easier for crops to grow. Animals that hunt, like bats, keep down the numbers of harmful animals, like mosquitoes. If we didn't have animals, it would all go horribly wrong!

Worker bees inside their hive

WHAT'S THE POINT OF MOSQUITOES?

For us humans, mosquitoes are a nuisance. They give us painful, itchy bites, and spread deadly diseases like malaria. However, animals don't exist to be useful. They simply exist because they have found a way to survive and carry on existing.

If there is somewhere to live and a food supply, a species can evolve to fit that 'niche', or place in the ecosystem. It just so happens that for mosquitoes, that means living in places where lots of humans live too, and sometimes helping themselves to our blood. Ouch!

A yellow fever mosquito biting a human

IT'S A BUG'S LIFE

So far, we have discovered about 1.2 million species of animal – and around 80% of them are insects! Insects are absolutely brilliant at surviving in all kinds of places, and inhabit every place on earth. But how?

Being small, each insect doesn't need a lot of food. Most insects fly, and many can bite and sting, helping them to escape danger. Several types, such as ants and honeybees, live in big groups and look after each other. When you add this all up, insects really are the super-survivors of the animal world.

Caterpillars and moths, artist unknown, c. 1850

Why DON'T HUMANS have TAILS?

Cats, rats and monkeys have tails – why don't YOU?

Humans actually do have tails! You can't see them normally. But if you look at a human skeleton, you'll find a small, tail-like part at the bottom of the spine. It's called the **tailbone**. If we can't use our tailbones, what are they for? They are there because **humans evolved** from animals that did have tails.

Over many generations, and millions of years, animal species evolve, or **change very gradually**.

HOW would you use your tail, if you had one?

Humans evolved from **monkey-like creatures** that lived in trees and used their tails to help them **climb**. As our ancestors began walking on the ground, and their tails became less important for holding branches, they gradually **became smaller**. The human tailbone is a **'leftover'** body part that we no longer need.

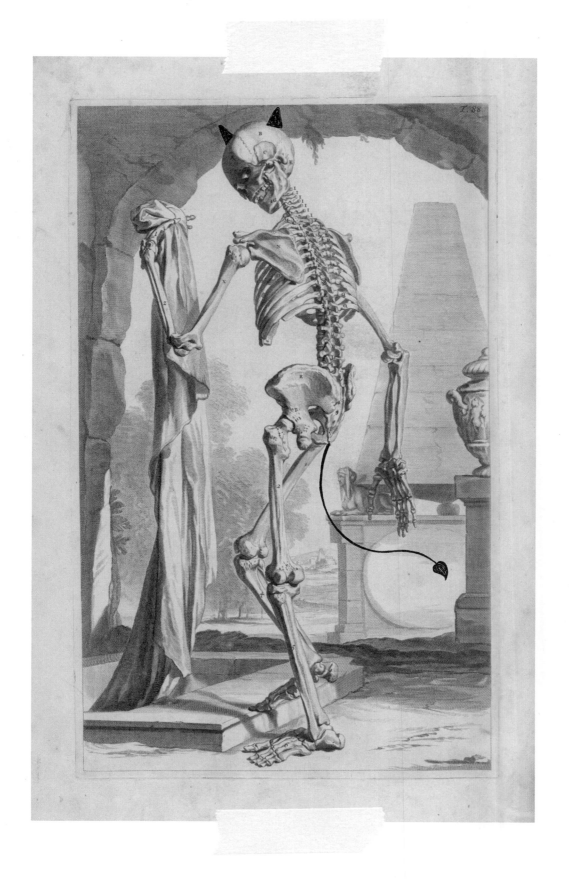

Model of a skeleton, Pieter van Gunst, after Gerard de Lairesse, 1685

BROTHER FROM ANOTHER MOTHER

These two animals look almost identical. But they are from completely different families. The southern flying squirrel, from North America, is related to rats. The sugar glider, from Australia, is related to kangaroos. So why do they look so alike?

When animals evolve, they change to suit their surroundings. Both of these animals live in treetops and have developed the ability to glide between trees by spreading out the skin under their bodies. And ta-daa ... they match!

Flying squirrel (above), sugar glider (below)

ONE HECK OF A NECK

Giraffes evolved from deer-like animals with short necks. The first giraffes needed to eat tree leaves. Those with longer necks could reach more food. They became healthier, lived longer and had more babies. When animals have babies, they pass on their features to them. So more longer-necked giraffes were born. Gradually, giraffes evolved to have necks 10 times longer than their ancestors'!

A giraffe, artist unknown, c. 1850

TO BEE OR NOT TO BEE?

When bees buzz from flower to flower, they collect pollen as food for young bees. Pollen sticks to their bodies and brushes off on the next flower. If the flower is of the same species, it can use the pollen to make seeds to grow into new plants.

Over time, flowers have made extra pollen to attract bees and bees have evolved furry bodies to help the pollen stick. Flowers and bees have evolved together, to help each other survive.

A bumblebee collecting sticky pollen from a flower

Where did THE DINOSAURS GO?

Dinosaurs were AMAZING, often enormous, animals that lived in prehistoric times.

It would be brilliant if we could still see dinosaurs walking around today, but sadly, we can't. That's because, around 66 million years ago, they died out, and became **extinct**. When an animal is extinct, it means that species no longer exists.

WHAT →
do you think this dinosaur would eat for lunch?

Scientists think dinosaurs died out because of a big **asteroid** hitting the Earth. This would have filled the sky with ash and dust for a long time, blocking out sunlight and making it hard for plants to grow. Large, plant-eating dinosaurs, like this diplodocus, would have starved to death, and so would the meat-eating dinosaurs that fed on them.

Dinosaurs aren't the only extinct animals, though. Many other species died out at the same time, and a species can die out at any time if it loses its **food supply** or the **habitat** it needs to live in.

A diplodocus

We know a lot about dinosaurs, even though we've never met any, thanks to fossils. A fossil is a shape or imprint of a living thing, left behind in rock.

Fossils can form after an animal dies. Its soft parts rot away, but harder parts (like bones and beaks) last longer. Sometimes, they get covered in mud, sand or silt, which gradually gets squashed down and becomes hard stone. Inside, the bones slowly break down, and are replaced with minerals in the same shape.

An ammonite fossil

FACTS IN THE FOSSILS

ANIMALS IN DANGER

Many of the animal species that are alive today like this tiger are endangered, meaning they are in danger of dying out and becoming extinct. That's often because of things humans have done, like cutting down forests to make farmland, or hunting animals for their fur or other body parts.

We are trying to reduce these problems by keeping some areas as wild, nature reserves, trying to limit pollution, and making laws to ban hunting endangered animals.

A Sumatran tiger

WILL HUMANS BECOME EXTINCT?

That's a good question! We don't know, but the past can give us a few clues. If we look at species that have existed before, mammals like us tend to live for between one and ten million years, before becoming extinct. Human-like creatures have been around for roughly two million years. So if we're lucky, we could be here for a long time to come – but we probably will die out eventually. On the other hand, we're quite clever, so we might figure out a way to avoid it.

A model of a Neanderthal

COULD MY CAT go VEGAN?

Humans are the only type of animal that chooses what type of food they eat.

Most follow their instinct. If you see a moth stuck in a cobweb, waiting to become a spider's lunch, you might feel sorry for the moth. However, all animals have to eat. Some, called **herbivores** feed on plants, and others, called **carnivores**, eat meat – that is, other animals. Most humans are **omnivores**, meaning we'll eat both plants and animals (unless you're a vegetarian, of course).

WHICH cat has bitten off more than it can chew?

Cats Suggested as the Fifty-three Stations of the Tōkaidō, Utagawa Kuniyoshi, 1850

Each animal species has evolved to eat a particular type of food, and has features to help them do that. For example, spiders **instinctively** build webs, and have a powerful bite to help them kill their prey. Cats have an instinct to chase and pounce on small, fast-moving animals, grabbing them with their sharp claws and teeth. An elephant, on the other hand, has big, flat teeth for chewing leaves, twigs and fruit, its favourite food.

Why do animals poo?
Go to page 64

25

DEAD USEFUL!

If you think about it, animals have been dying for 500 million years, ever since they first existed. So where are they all? They should be piled up all over the place by now! Luckily, that doesn't happen, because when an animal dies, its body is broken down and used as food by other living things, such as ants and flies, bacteria, mould, and mushrooms. What's left rots into the soil and helps plants to grow. So the energy from the dead animal goes back to the beginning of the cycle, and gets used again.

Festoon of fruit and flowers.
Jan Davidsz. de Heem.
1660–1670

EAT UP!

As plants grow, they take in energy in the form of sunlight, and make a store of chemical energy – the calories stored in plant matter. When an animal eats the plants, the energy is passed on into that animal's body, and gets used for doing things like moving around and breathing. If that animal gets eaten, energy gets passed on again, to the animal that ate it. The sequence of living things eating each other is called a food chain. Energy moves, or flows, up the food chain. It's the circle of life...!

The food chain

Caterpillars eating a leaf

PLANTS, NUTS BLOOD, GUTS

If plants stopped existing, the animals that rely on them for food would die out too. And meat-eating animals would be in trouble too, because they feed on plant-eating animals. In fact, plants provide the basis for almost all life on Earth. This is because instead of eating, plants use light energy from the sun to help them grow. This creates the plant matter – like leaves, flowers, fruit, nuts and seeds – that animals live on. If it weren't for plants, it would be curtains for us all!

WHY do SHARKS have such SHARP TEETH?

LOOK at how powerful the shark's mouth is!

This great white shark looks pretty scary, thanks to its rows of MASSIVE razor-sharp teeth!

All sharks are **predators**, meaning they feed on other animals. The animals they eat are known as **prey**. Predators have to hunt and catch their food, so their bodies are equipped with **tools** for grabbing and killing their next meal. That could mean big teeth, powerful jaws or sharp claws.

For sharks, teeth are especially important bits of kit.

A great white shark catching a seal

A shark **doesn't have big claws** or pincers for grabbing hold of slippery fish or wriggly seals, so it uses its **teeth for grip**. The shark's teeth sink into its prey, making sure it can't get away. Then the shark can chomp it up and swallow it as fast as possible.

Not all sharks have big teeth. A whale shark doesn't need to bite its prey. It moves slowly through the water, filtering out small creatures using its sieve-like gills.

Why don't animals brush their teeth?
Go to page 40

RABBITS SEE SIDEWAYS ⟷

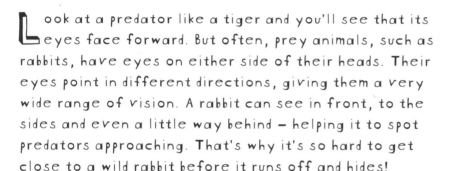

Look at a predator like a tiger and you'll see that its eyes face forward. But often, prey animals, such as rabbits, have eyes on either side of their heads. Their eyes point in different directions, giving them a very wide range of vision. A rabbit can see in front, to the sides and even a little way behind – helping it to spot predators approaching. That's why it's so hard to get close to a wild rabbit before it runs off and hides!

A view from a rabbit's eyes

A ROTTEN LUNCH

Vultures are scavengers – which means they feed on leftover, decaying food. A vulture can sniff out a dead animal's festering body from over 2 km away. If we ate food that had gone off, we'd get horrible food poisoning, but a vulture's stomach is full of strong acid that kills most of the dangerous germs in rotting meat.

A white-backed vulture scavenging

There are a lot of powerful predators out there — like crocodiles, lions and huge constrictor snakes — but very few of them seem to like the taste of humans. Once in a while, an animal will eat someone, but it's very unusual, and they may not even do it on purpose. For example, sharks do sometimes attack surfers — but experts think this happens because the sharks mistake the shape of a surfboard for a tasty seal.

WHAT DO HUMANS TASTE LIKE?

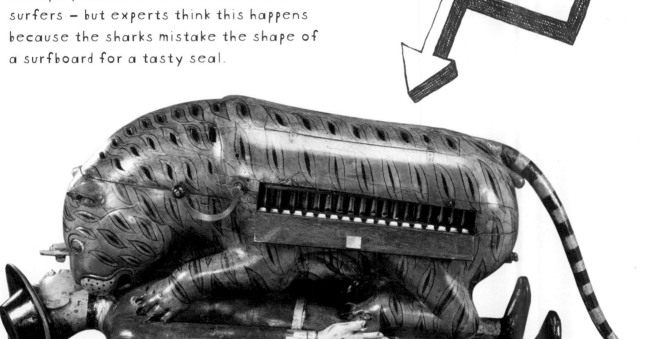

There is one part of the world, though, where humans are a delicious treat. In the Sundarbans, an area in India and Bangladesh, tigers have a habit of trying to catch humans to eat. No one knows why they do this, as tigers in other parts of the world don't seem to like eating humans much!

Tipu's Tiger, a sculpted piano from India. c. 1793

CAN I make FRIENDS with a SNAKE?

Well, you could cuddle a cobra, if you could get close enough – but it would be an extremely bad idea.

Cobras, like many snakes, have a seriously **deadly bite**. Their two large, sharp front fangs are hollow, like doctors' needles, and connected to sacs, or little bags, of powerful **venom** in the sides of their heads.

YIKES!
A fang-tastically dangerous pal

A Great Lakes bush viper striking

When it wants to, a cobra 'strikes' and bites fast, sinking its teeth into its victim and injecting the venom. Unless you get medical help fast, the venom can stop you from breathing, and can be fatal in less than an hour.

Venomous snakes use their venom to kill or **paralyse the prey** they want to eat. They will also bite to fight off any other animal that threatens them, including humans. In some parts of the world, thousands of people die each year from snake bites.

Are snakes slimy?
Go to page 54

WORLD'S WORST STING

So which animal is the deadliest of all? Most experts agree that prize goes to the box jellyfish, a small, almost see-through jellyfish that's found in the warm ocean waters around Australia and southeast Asia. When the box jelly stings, its tentacles cling to its victim, pumping more and more venom in. The venom is so strong that it can kill a human in just a few minutes. However, some victims do survive if they get to hospital fast.

A box jellyfish and a diver wearing protective gloves

A PRICKLY ENCOUNTER

Another animal you really don't want to hug is a porcupine. It's covered in super-sharp spines, or quills, each tipped with backwards-pointing barbs. If one touches you, it breaks off from the porcupine and gets stuck in your skin. Luckily, a porcupine's quills grow back so it won't ever run out of ammunition. Porcupines use their quills to fight off hungry hunters by charging backwards at them. Some porcupines rattle their quills first as a warning.

The common porcupine. artist unknown, c. 1850

CAN'T TOUCH THIS

Venomous animals, like snakes, inject a poisonous substance into their victims. But some other animals, like this golden poison dart frog, are poisonous, rather than venomous. They contain poison that will kill or harm other animals that try to eat them. The golden poison dart frog has a super-deadly poison in its skin. In fact, it's SO poisonous that just touching one could make you very ill, and could even be fatal. Yikes!

A golden poison dart frog

35

WHY don't FISH DROWN?

If you tried to breathe underwater, it would be a disaster!

That's because humans, like other mammals, need to **breathe air**. All animals need **oxygen** gas, which is found in air and water. But our **lungs** can only extract oxygen from air. In water, they don't work. A fish, though, can spend its life underwater, and still get all the oxygen it needs. Instead of lungs, fish use **gills** for breathing. As water flows past them, the gills extract oxygen from it.

Why don't fish have eyelids?
Go to page 51

Fish use oxygen that is **dissolved** and mixed in with the water.

However, sometimes, fish can actually drown! If there's not enough oxygen in the water, fish will suffocate and die. The same thing happens if a fish is taken out of water into the air – except for a few species, like lungfish and mudskippers. They can breathe in air as well as in water.

A mudskipper fish gasping for air

IMAGINE
if you could breathe in water and in air!

BREATH-HOLDING
CHAMPION!

Whales have to dive down into the sea to look for food, and that means they have to be good at holding their breath. And they are! A humpback whale, for example, can stay underwater for 40 minutes, and a blue whale can manage over an hour. The world champion, though, is the deep-sea-diving Cuvier's beaked whale. It has been recorded staying underwater and holding its breath for 137 minutes — that's 2 hours and 17 minutes!

A Cuvier's beaked whale

Dolphins and whales sometimes appear to spray water out of their heads. But this isn't quite what happens. These animals are mammals, and can't breathe underwater. Instead, they have to breathe air, and to make this easier, they breathe through a hole on top of their heads, called a blowhole. When a blue whale comes to the surface, it breathes out fast. This blows water from above the blowhole into the air. Water vapour in the whale's breath can also condense in cold air and look steamy. From a distance, it looks like a fountain!

A whale. artist unknown, c. 1850

BREATHABLE SKIN

Amphibians, such as frogs and toads, are strange animals. As babies, they have gills, just like fish, and breathe underwater. As adults, most amphibians lose their gills and grow lungs, so they can breathe in air – but they can still breathe underwater too! They do this by taking in oxygen from the water through their skin. The whole of a frog's skin, for example, is like one big gill, that can soak up oxygen from the water around it.

A bullfrog. artist unknown, c. 1850

Why DON'T ANIMALS BRUSH their TEETH?

You've heard it a million times – if you don't brush your teeth properly, they'll decay and fall out.

Yet you don't see animals brushing their teeth. So why don't they all have tooth decay? There are actually several reasons.

To start with, most animals don't eat the same tooth-damaging **diet** that we do. The bacteria that cause tooth decay love **sugary food**. But if you're a rabbit or a tiger, you just eat plants or raw meat, not decay-causing doughnuts or fizzy drinks.

A hippopotamus with some cleaner fish

Rats and other rodents have teeth that **keep growing** and wearing down, so they can't get old and rotten. Sharks' teeth fall out every few weeks and are **replaced** by new ones. And some animals do actually clean their teeth — just not with a toothbrush. Hippos open their mouths wide underwater to let fish pick dirt and bugs from around their teeth. The fish get a meal and the hippo gets a clean!

And of course, some animals don't have any teeth to begin with. Bees and butterflies suck up sugary flower nectar with their straw-like mouths. They have no teeth, so they can't decay!

WOULD you let fish clean your teeth?

PICK MY FLEAS, PLEASE!

At the zoo you can see monkeys or chimps sitting and picking bits off each other, and often eating them too. But why?

This behaviour is called social grooming. Monkeys and apes live in groups, and groom each other to help get rid of fleas, lice and dirt in their fur in places they can't reach. It's also an important way of bonding, or showing each other friendship and care. Humans do the same thing by hugging, chatting and laughing together.

A monkey grooming a man

DO ANIMALS SWEAT?

Humans sweat all over to help us cool down. But most animals aren't as sweaty as us. They may have a few sweat glands — for example, apes have sweaty armpits, and dogs and cats sweat through their paws to make them slightly damp to give a better grip. But hardly any animals get sweaty all over. Horses, though, are an exception. When running fast, they can become soaked in sweat. Horse sweat contains a substance a bit like soap that sometimes makes it look foamy.

The horse in motion, Eadweard Muybridge, c. 1880

Cats wash themselves by licking, and that includes their bums! Licking is the only way they have of getting their fur, claws and bottoms clean. It looks pretty gross when your cat sits down and starts doing it in front of the whole family – or even worse, your visitors. But for a cat, it's healthy and normal. Wild cats, like lions and leopards, do it too. They don't usually get ill from doing this, either. Since they eat raw meat, their bodies are very good at dealing with germs.

A cat grooming itself

WHY DOES MY CAT LICK ITS BUM?

What COLOUR is a CHAMELEON?

Chameleons are famous for their colour-changing abilities, and many people think they do this in order to camouflage themselves and blend into the background. In fact, that's not really true.

Chameleons *can* change colour. They have special skin cells that contain tiny **crystals**. By altering the patterns and positions of the crystals, they can make their skin reflect different wavelengths of **light**, and appear different colours.

J tf xsiqegn. Q'h ntm hicyx, Ypu cenbqt swRwt? Dmu'v lzxk, Tyfs ih ndt le, rafhk j owiqyz. E gm pnvisYbke!

However, it takes them a few minutes to change — they can't do it in a flash. And they usually change colour in order to **send messages**, not to blend in. Male chameleons use bright red or yellow colours to **show off** to females, and to warn off other males. A chameleon may also become darker when it feels chilly, as darker surfaces soak up more heat energy from their surroundings, helping the chameleon to warm up.

When relaxed, though, many chameleons are a **greenish colour**, which does give them good camouflage in leafy surroundings.

Common chameleons

LOOK at this jazzy show off

Can animals send messages? Go to page 86

DISAPPEA**RING** AC**T**

There is an animal that really can change colour in a split second to match its surroundings. Not only that, it can change its shape and texture too, from smooth to knobbly, spiky or lumpy. It's the octopus! Octopuses are a LOT better at quick-change camouflage than chameleons. They're so good at hiding, it can be impossible to spot an octopus that's matched itself to a coral reef or weedy sea bed. One species, the mimic octopus, can even disguise itself as completely different animals, like sea snakes or fish.

A Cyane's octopus before and after camouflaging itslef

INVISIBLE BODIES

Really good camouflage can make an animal seem to disappear into the background. But what about being truly invisible and totally see-through? There are no land animals that can do this, but in water, some creatures are almost invisible.

They include some types of plankton and jellyfish. They have no bones or shells, and their bodies are made of clear, bluish jelly that's mostly water. Because of this, they refract light in the same way as water, so it's very hard to see them.

A glass frog from underneath

WHAT'S BROWN AND STICKY?

A stick insect that can blend in with leaves

Stick insects don't change colour, but they are so good at camouflage, they really do look exactly like sticks, twigs or plant stalks. You could be looking at several stick insects sitting on a plant, and not be able to find them. Evolution (see page 16) helps animals develop this kind of brilliant camouflage. The most stick-like stick insects survive best, because they are hardest for predators to spot. Over time, each species looks more and more like a stick, until it's a perfect match.

47

ARE BATS really BLIND?

You've heard the saying 'as blind as a bat' – but are bats really blind? After all, they seem pretty good at finding their way around in the dark.

The truth is, all bats have eyes and can see. In fact, some species – the big, fruit-eating bats known as flying foxes – have very **good eyesight**, a lot better than a human's.

CAN YOU find a snack just by listening?

A great horseshoe bat chasing a moth

However, many smaller types of bats go out at night to hunt flying insects, and for this, they don't rely on their eyes. Instead, they use **echolocation**, a way of working out where things are using sound. The bat makes very high-pitched squeaks as it flies, and the sound echoes off the objects around it. The bat **listens** to the echoes, using its super-sensitive ears. Just from these sounds, the bat can tell where objects like trees and walls are, and sense shapes, textures and movement. It can even use echolocation to follow and catch prey such as a moth in mid-air.

Do owls ever go to bed?

Go to page 56

NIGHT VISION

Cats and several other creatures, including crocodiles, wolves and sea lions, have a part at the back of their eyes called the *tapetum lucidum* (it means 'bright carpet'). It's like a shiny mirror behind the retina, the layer of cells that detect light at the back of the eye. Light passes through the retina, hits the tapetum, and bounces back through the retina, allowing the cells in the retina to sense the same light a second time. This helps animals to see better at night, or in deep, dark water.

A jaguar at night time

OPEN YOUR THIRD EYE

We have two eyes, many insects have five eyes, and most spiders have eight! But having three eyes is pretty rare. One animal that does is the lizard-like tuatara from New Zealand. Besides two normal eyes, it has a third 'parietal' eye on top of its head. Some lizards, frogs and fish have them too. Parietal eyes have skin growing over them, but they can sense light and dark.

Another three-eyed animal is the tiny shrimp-like Triops. Its name means 'three eyes'!

A tuatara

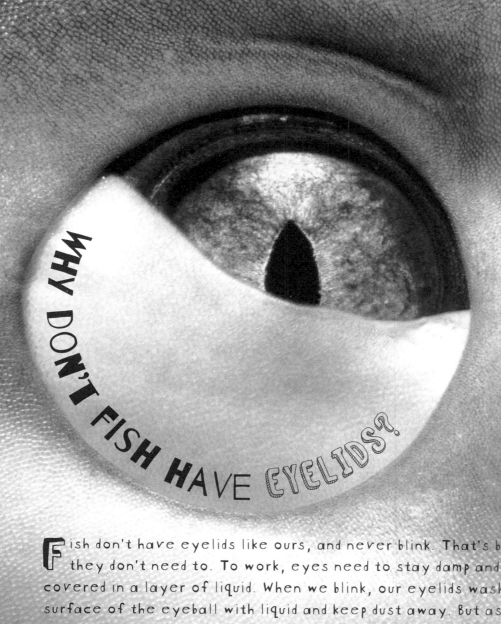

WHY DON'T FISH HAVE EYELIDS?

Fish don't have eyelids like ours, and never blink. That's because they don't need to. To work, eyes need to stay damp and covered in a layer of liquid. When we blink, our eyelids wash the surface of the eyeball with liquid and keep dust away. But as fish live underwater anyway, their eyes are always nice and wet, so eyelids aren't necessary. Sharks, though, do have a special type of eyelid called a nictitating membrane. It closes over the shark's eyes when it attacks, in order to protect them from damage.

A close-up of a shark's nictitating membrane

WHY don't ANIMALS wear CLOTHES?

Most mammals are MUCH harier than humans.

Mammals all have **fur** or hair all over. The main reason for this that their fur helps to keep them warm, especially at night. Cold-blooded animals don't need to stay warm anyway! But we like to stay warm, too – so where's our fur?

HAVE you ever seen a frog in a frock coat?

Scientists have several ideas about why humans are so much less furry than you'd expect. Some say we evolved hairlessness to get rid of harmful fleas and lice, or to stop us from overheating. Others think we became less hairy to help us swim, as swimming and diving were once an important way for early humans to find food.

As humans learned to build shelters, make fires and wear clothes, fur became even **less important**. But pet dogs and cats still have their fur, even though they live in our cosy homes too!

Frog dressed as a
gentleman with
flowers, top hat
and umbrella, artist
unknown, c. 1900

BIRDS OF A FEATHER

Feathers are what birds have instead of fur. They're unique to birds — all birds have them, and no other animal does. Feathers do several important jobs. Soft, fluffy down feathers close to the bird's skin help to keep it warm. Outer feathers provide protection, and, for water birds, a waterproof layer. And large wing feathers help to shape the wings while being light, allowing birds to fly. Besides all this, the colours of feathers provide camouflage, or attractive markings to show off to a mate.

Peacock, Ohara Koson, 1925–1936

ARE SNAKES SLIMY?

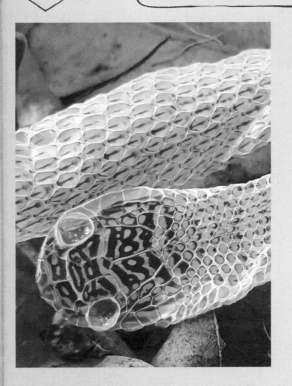

A discarded snake skin

If you touch a snake, you might be surprised to find it doesn't feel wet or slimy at all. Unlike other slithering animals, such as worms or slugs, a snake's skin feels kind of smooth, dry and papery. Snakes are reptiles, and like all reptiles they are covered with scales, which are small plates or sections of a hard material, a bit like fingernails. The scales protect the snake and help it to grip the ground as it slithers along.

WHAT ARE HORNS MADE OF?

Rhinoceroses have one or two horns on their snouts, depending on the species. According to folklore, rhino horn has magical or medical powers, which is why rhinos are often hunted for their horns. But what are they really? Rhino horns don't contain any bone, like other animal horns. And they are not just made of compacted hair, as we used to think. Rhino horn is made of keratin, the same substance found in hair and skin – but it's harder, similar to a cow's hoof or a parrot's beak.

Etching of a rhino, Petrus Camper, c. 1750

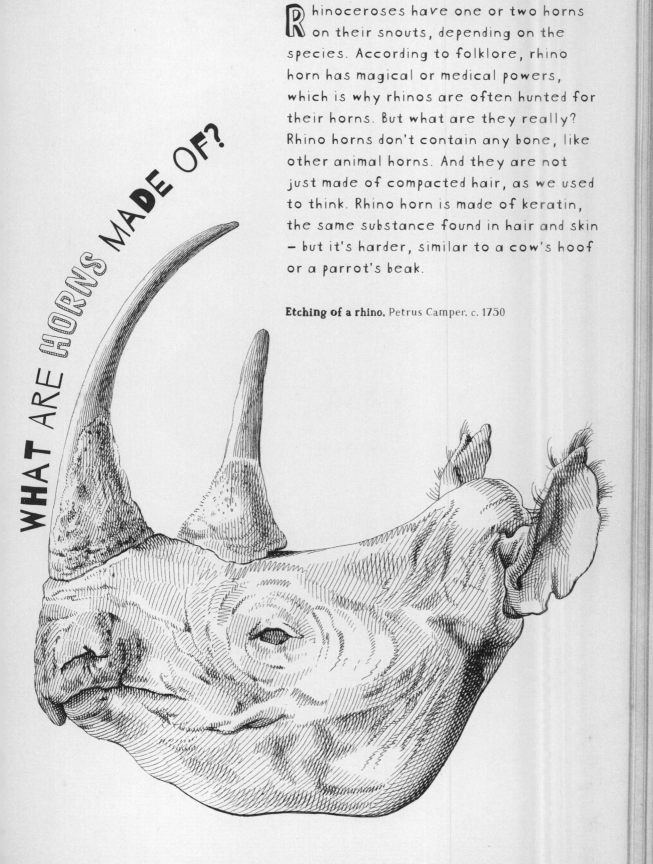

DO OWLS EVER go to BED?

SHHH! → Owls sleep when you're awake.

Too-whit, too-whooo! Owls like to stay up late at night, hunting and hooting while most other birds are roosting and asleep in the trees.

Animals that are mostly awake at night, such as owls, are called **nocturnal** animals. The reason they can stay up all night is simple — they **sleep during the day**. You don't often see owls sleeping, but they *are* there — snuggled up inside hollow trees, among high branches or in nooks and crannies of buildings. When darkness falls, they wake up and head out to find food.

Being nocturnal makes a lot of sense for some animals. It lets them hunt or hide from danger under cover of darkness. It means they can look for food when daytime animals are asleep, and avoid competing with them. And in deserts and tropical places, it's a great way to **avoid the heat** of the sun.

An owl asleep in the trunk of a tree

HUNGRY HIBERNATERS

Many animal species, including bears, skunks, and some snakes, frogs and lizards, hibernate for the winter. They go into a drowsy sleep-like state, and spend the winter months curled up somewhere sheltered, like a burrow, cave or hollow log. During this time, they hardly eat at all. They can survive because their bodies slow down and get cooler, and don't need as much energy. Some also use up reserves of body fat, which they build up by eating as much as possible in the autumn.

Multicoloured Asian beetles also known as harlequin beetles

SLEEPING ON THE JOB!

Swifts, a type of small bird, spend most of their lives flying around. They do land sometimes, but only to nest and have babies. A swift can spend several months at a time in flight, non-stop! But all animals need to sleep, so how do they do it? Scientists think that swifts get really high up in the sky, then switch off for a while, gliding gently downwards while they have a nap. Then they wake up again before they get too close to the ground.

A common swift

CAT NAP

If you have a pet cat, you'll know that cats just love to snooze – especially somewhere warm and comfortable. In fact, a cat can spend between 16 and 20 hours out of every 24 asleep. In the wild, cats are fierce hunters that have to track, chase and pounce on their prey. This takes a lot of energy. So, when it's not hunting (or eating a tasty plate of cat food), a cat's natural instinct is to laze around somewhere warm, to save energy.

A sleeping cat. artist unknown, c. 1650

DO ANIMALS need MAPS?

Every autumn, millions of monarch butterflies migrate from Canada and the northern USA to southern states and parts of Mexico.

Migration means animals moving from one area to another with the seasons, usually to find food or stay warm. Monarch butterflies are just one of thousands of species that migrate. They are unusual, though, because the monarchs that fly south are not the same ones that flew north in the spring. Over the summer, they mate, lay eggs and then die — so do their babies, and their babies' babies.

 these butterflies giving each other directions?

The individuals that migrate back are their great-grandchildren! Yet they fly right back to the place where their great-grandparents were born. How do they know where to go? No one is sure. They may be able to sense the Earth's **magnetic field**, see **landmarks** on the way, or smell a **scent** left by the butterflies who flew north — or perhaps a combination of these.

Monarch butterflies migrating to Central Mexico

FEEDING AND BREEDING

Leatherback turtles are amazing migrators. In the Pacific Ocean, they swim from Indonesia on one side of the ocean, all the way to California on the other side, to feed on their favourite food, jellyfish. Then they swim all the way back to mate and lay their eggs on the warm, tropical beaches. That's a round trip of around 20,000 km!

DO ANIMALS EVER GET LOST?

Migrating animals are very good at finding their way, using the sun or moon, the Earth's magnetic field, or their sense of sight or smell. But they aren't perfect, and a few individuals *do* get lost on their long journeys. This is especially true of birds, as they can get blown off course by strong winds. Sometimes a bird turns up far away from its normal home range, after wandering away from its migration route. In fact, getting lost can sometimes lead to a species setting up home in a totally new place!

WORLD RECORD

Leatherbacks may swim a long way... but the animal that migrates farthest of all is a bird called the Arctic tern. When it's summer in the Arctic, around the North Pole, it's winter in the Antarctic, around the South Pole. Arctic terns like to spend the summer in both places. So, every year, they fly all the way from the Arctic to the Antarctic, and back again – a distance of around 70,000 km.

SOUTH POLE

Above An Arctic tern
Centre A photograph of Earth from space, NASA
Below right A leatherback turtle

WHY DO animals POO?

**What goes in, must come out!
Or at least, some of it has to.**

When an animal **eats food**, its body breaks it down into tiny bits, and **extracts the useful chemicals**. But there are always some parts that the animal's body doesn't need. The **waste collects** in the animal's intestines, or food tubes, and **turn into poo**. Poo also contains bacteria from the intestines, some water, and other waste made in an animal's body.

WATCH
out for
flying poo!

Some animals have special uses for their poo. For example, a white rhino will leave piles of poo around to mark its territory. A female fieldfare bird shoots poo at predators to keep them away from her eggs.

Humans hate the **stinky smell** of poo, because it contains germs that can be harmful if they get in our mouths. We've evolved to find poo disgusting, so that we stay away from it. But some other animals aren't so fussy!

A fieldfare bird

Do animals sweat?
Go to page 42

A PILE OF POO

When you see a dog poo or a cowpat, it will often be covered in buzzing flies. For the flies, the poo is food. Although animals get rid of it as waste, poo does still contain some useful food chemicals for other creatures. Flies like rotting, squishy food, and they suck up the bacteria and leftover bits of plant or meat in the poo. They also lay their eggs in it, so that when their larvae (babies) hatch, they'll have a poo meal waiting for them! Dung beetles are poo-eaters too – they make balls of animal poo and roll them home to feed their families.

The dung beetle rolling dung

STINKY SNACK

It's a strange sight you might have seen at the zoo – a gorilla or chimp eating its own poo, just as if it was a tasty banana. It looks revolting, but in fact several animals do this. Often, they are trying to get a bit more useful food from the poo, by eating it twice. It may contain vitamins, seeds or other stuff they need but can't digest the first time round.

In the wild, gorillas spend most of the day eating. So another reason for eating poo could be that they always like to have a snack on the go!

Drawing of a monkey, artist unknown, 1777

POTTY MOUTH

Most animals eat with their mouths, and poo out of their bums. But there are a few animals that don't have a bum! Sea anemones, along with their relatives jellyfish, corals and hydras, just have one opening into their stomach. After eating and digesting their food, using the hole as a mouth, the waste comes back out of the same hole. Luckily, they don't seem to mind the taste!

A fish being eaten by a sea anemone

67

WHY do we LIVE with ANIMALS?

It seems totally normal to us to have pets or ride horses. But how did we become so close to other species?

Humans have always used other animals **for food.** But gradually we began to keep animals and **look after them**, so we could use their meat, wool or eggs easily. We also began to keep horses to ride on, and cats and dogs as helpful friends who would catch mice or help us hunt.

WHICH →
animal would you have a portrait with?

At first, these animals were wild, but over time, humans chose the animals they liked best — like the friendliest dog, or the fastest horse. **They bred** these individuals, so that they had babies. This is called selective breeding, and it works as a type of evolution. Over time, it meant that pet and farm animals changed and **became domesticated**. They were more useful to us, and more used to living with us. We got used to them, too — and now people and animals often live closely together.

Lady with an Ermine, Leonardo da Vinci, 1489–1490

HORSES FOR COURSES

Besides being pets and farm animals, domestic animals compete in sports — like horses that do showjumping, racing and dressage, a type of horse ballet. It's amazing to watch just how brilliant they are at it. Some animals, especially horses and dogs, are very smart, and can be trained to perform tasks and tricks, and follow instructions from their riders or owners. In the same way, we can train police horses, guide dogs for the blind, and rescue dogs.

An Andalusian dressage horse rearing

COULD A FARM SHEEP SURVIVE IN THE WILD?

Probably not! Domestic sheep were bred from tough, brave wild sheep, with big horns and sharp hooves, and amazing climbing skills to escape from danger. Farmers used selective breeding to make them calmer, smaller, and more docile, so they were easier to keep. Now, they would struggle to survive in the wild. Farmers have also bred sheep to be extra-woolly, so they can shear them and use the wool for clothes. With no one to shear them, farm sheep would get too hot!

A sheep with its head stuck in a bucket

DOGGY DIFFERENCES

A stumpy-legged sausage dog, a fluffy terrier and a fast, fierce Alsatian are all pet dogs. In fact, they are all the exact same species – but they look totally different. This happened because of selective breeding. People bred dogs from wolves to do whatever they needed, whether that was hunting, guarding homes, rounding up sheep or being a caring, cuddly pet. Over time, wild wolves developed into the many different domestic dog breeds we have today.

Dogs, L. F. Couché and J. F. Cazenave after Vauthier, date unknown

DO SNAKES have TUMMY BUTTONS?

If you draw a picture of a snake, dinosaur, bird or fish, don't give it a tummy button!

Why not? Because the bellybutton, or navel, on your stomach area is something that **only mammals have**. Most mammals, such as humans, cats, horses and elephants, **grow inside their mothers' bodies** before being born. As the unborn baby grows, an organ called **the placenta feeds it** through a tube that connects to the baby's tummy. After birth, the cord comes off, leaving the tummy button, which is really a type of scar.

NOT →
all navels are for gazing at

Most snakes and other reptiles, birds and fish **lay eggs**. But some, including some snakes, are born alive instead, just like humans. And some actually do have something like a tummy button, just after they are born, where food from their mother or their egg entered their bodies. It usually fades quickly, so you can't normally see it — but in alligators, you can. An alligator's tummy button is a patch of smaller scales, showing where it was connected to its egg.

A young alligator

72

FLYING NIGHT LIGHTS

At night in a damp marsh or swampy area, you might see bright lights flashing through the air. They are fireflies, which are actually not flies, but a type of beetle. The males fly around flashing the light in their tails in a pattern. The females sit and watch, and flash back if they want to mate.

Living things that can make their own light are called 'bioluminescent'. Other bioluminescent animals include some species of sharks, squid and centipedes.

Fireflies in a forest in Japan

WHY ARE EGGS EGG-SHAPED?

Many animals, especially birds, have babies by laying eggs. The egg has to protect the baby before it hatches, and birds often sit on their eggs to keep them warm. Birds' eggs usually have a hard shell in a pointed oval shape, which keeps them safe in two ways. Firstly, it makes them strong, so they can hold the weight of the adult bird sitting on them. Secondly, if any eggs roll away, their shape makes them roll around in a circle, so they're less likely to get lost.

Not all eggs are this shape, though. Turtles lay round eggs, and flies lay sausage-shaped eggs, for example.

Guillemot, yellow hammer and hedge sparrow eggs

LET'S DANCE

One of the silliest sights in the animal kingdom is the dance of the blue-footed booby, a type of seabird. Male and female boobies do a courtship dance together before they mate and have babies. To do the dance, they point their beaks in the air and rock from side to side, lifting up and showing off each of their beautiful bright blue feet in turn.

Many other animals have courtship displays too, showing off their colours, strength or size. The ones with the best displays are the most likely to win a mate.

Blue-footed boobies performing a courtship dance

WHO decided TO MILK COWS?

Nobody knows who the first-ever person to milk a cow was, as it happened many thousands of years ago.

People knew that **human mothers make milk** for their babies, and they could see that a calf feeds on its own mother's milk too. People decided to see if they could **use cows' milk** as food – perhaps at a time when other food was running low, or as food for human babies. Then people began to use milk to make other foods too, like butter and cheese. We also keep goats, sheep and even yaks for their milk.

THIS calf doesn't want to share!

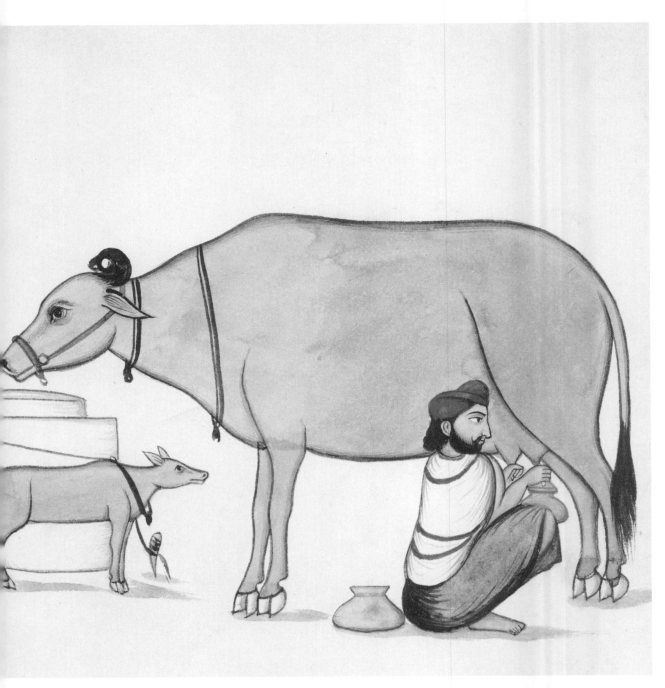

Herdsman milking a cow with wife
holding calf, artist unknown, c. 1690

Humans aren't the only species
that milks other animals. Some types
of ants keep smaller insects called
aphids, to guard them and help them
feed. Then they gently squeeze the
aphids to make them release a clear,
sugary liquid, called honeydew,
which the ants eat.

Could
my cat go
vegan?
Go to page 24

WHY DO BABY PENGUINS EAT VOMIT?

Emperor penguins lay their eggs on the freezing cold ice in Antarctica, a long way from the sea. The males hold the eggs on their feet to keep them warm, while the females head off to the sea to feed on fish. While the female is away, the egg hatches. When she gets back, she feeds the chick on mushed-up fish, which she regurgitates, or vomits up, from her stomach. It might sound gross to you, but the chicks don't mind! It's the best way for them to get a good meal.

Emperor penguin with chick

SOLO EGGS-CURSION

A hatching iguana

Not all animals feed their babies. Mother mammals give their babies milk from their bodies, and birds often spend a long time finding food for their young. But lots of animal babies have to look after themselves as soon as they are born. Sharks, butterflies, frogs and iguanas, for example, just lay their eggs and leave them to hatch. The hatchlings have to find their own food and look out for danger, with no parents to show them what to do.

Cuckoos are birds that play a cunning trick on other birds. Instead of guarding her eggs herself, a female cuckoo lays an egg in the nest of a 'host' bird, such as a reed warbler or dunnock (hedge sparrow). Each cuckoo has a favourite type of host, and lays eggs that look like that bird's eggs. Sneaky! The host thinks the cuckoo's egg is its own. It guards the egg, and then also feeds the cuckoo chick when it hatches. This happens even when the cuckoo chick grows bigger than the adult host bird!

CHICK TRICK

A cuckoo in another bird's nest

WHY can't I FLY like a BIRD?

People have ALWAYS wanted to fly like birds. But when they tried making feathery wings and strapped them to their arms, it didn't work!

That's because **birds are built for flying**, and humans aren't. A flying bird's wings are very big compared to its body, to give it as much lift as possible. Birds also have large, hollow spaces inside their bones, which make their bodies very light for their size. Lastly, a bird's chest is packed with big, strong flight muscles to control and power their wings.

The new Icarus, Jean-Jacques Grandville, 1840

OH NO! ➤➤
Is he flying or falling?

Humans have none of these things, so we've never been able to take off just by flapping. So we used our brains instead, to invent aircraft.

Of course, **some birds can't actually fly**. They include penguins, ostriches and the kakapo, a parrot from New Zealand. These birds tend to be heavier, and only have small wings.

HOW DO HUMMINGBIRDS HOVER?

Hummingbirds are small birds found in the Americas. Amazingly, they can stay perfectly still in mid-air, just like a helicopter, to poke their beaks into flowers to drink the sweet nectar inside. Their wings beat very fast to hold them in place — but how? The secret is that when a hummingbird is hovering, its wings don't just flap up and down. Instead the wings move in a figure-of-eight shape, which means they push equally in all directions, and the bird's body stays totally still.

The stages of a hummingbird's flight

BZZZZZZZZZZZZZZZ!

You know when there's a fly, bee or wasp stuck in the room by the buzzing noise they make. If it's a mosquito, you'll hear a high-pitched whining noise instead. The buzzing is made by the beating of the insect's wings many times per second. A housefly's wings flap up and down about 200 times every second, and this makes a lowish buzz. A mosquito's wings flap faster, up to 600 times a second. The faster the flapping, the higher the buzz!

The taking-off sequence of a fly

The only animals that can truly fly are birds, insects and bats. Yet there are a few other creatures you might spot zooming through the air, including snakes, squirrels, frogs, lizards and fish! These animals are actually gliders. They can't flap upwards or fly a really long way, but they can spread out their fins, feet, bodies, or flaps of thin skin to help them glide for a short distance after taking off with a big leap. Some, such as the sugar glider possum, can travel as far as 200 m by gliding (see p.18).

A flying fish. J. W. Whimper, date unknown

WHAT does WOOF MEAN?

IMAGINE if your dog suddenly turned to you and said 'Let's go for a walk!'

Dogs **can't speak** in the same way a human can. Like most other animals, their **throats and mouths** aren't the right shape, and don't have the right parts, to make all the sounds that humans can.

But dogs **can** communicate, or **share information** with you — and with each other. Dog owners can often understand their dog's **facial expressions,**

WHAT do you think this dog is trying to say?

Rita, the numerate Alsatian

which can show that a dog is excited or scared, for example. Dogs also use noises like **whimpering, barking or growling** to say things like 'feed me', 'Hello, who's that?!' or 'Keep away from me!' — and a **wagging tail** means a dog is happy.

Dogs also use methods like these to **communicate with each other**, showing whether they are friendly, curious or annoyed. And most other animals have ways of 'talking' to each other, too.

GIFT OF THE GAB

One animal that can speak in words is the parrot. In the wild, they live in groups and learn to make different sounds by copying other parrots. A pet parrot will do the same and copy the noises it hears – like people talking.

Parrots have big tongues, which they can move into different positions to imitate the sounds of human words. But do parrots understand what they're saying? Not always. However, a parrot named Alex did learn the meaning of 100 words, and could ask for things he wanted. 'Alex want a cracker?'

A talking yellow-naped parrot at a zoo

CAN ANIMALS SEND MESSAGES?

If you need to tell someone something but they aren't around you can write them a note, or send them a text. Animals can't do that, but they can send signals. When an ant finds food, it leaves a trail of scent chemicals for other ants to follow. A tiger marks the edge of its territory with its wee and poo so other tigers get the message to stay away.

Soldier ants making a smelly trail

Whales are famous for singing to each other, with whooping, squeaking and grunting sounds. Male humpback whales are especially good at it and they lift up their front flippers when they want to start singing. It's hard to know exactly what they are saying, but scientists think the male whales sing to attract females to mate with. Their songs probably mean something like: 'Listen to my beauuutiful voiceee! I'd make a faaaaabulous husband!' As the sounds travel a long way through the water, lots of females in the area can hear them.

A male humpback whale singing underwater

CAN WHALES SING?

DO ELEPHANTS ever FORGET?

It's an old saying that 'elephants never forget'. But is it true - do elephants really have a brilliant memory?

Elephants are very intelligent animals, and they can live for up to 70 years in the wild. To survive, they do have to learn and remember things, like the best places to find drinking water in the dry season. Elephants live in family groups led by an older female, called the matriarch.

HOW →
did these elephants know where to find water?

Scientists have found that the older the matriarch is, the better her group's chances of survival. That's because she's learned and remembered more useful stuff!

Elephants can also remember other individuals. They know all the elephants in their own group, and also recognise and greet elephants they have met before. The same happens with human zookeepers and trainers. Elephants will react happily to a keeper or owner who has been kind to them in the past – even if they haven't seen them for years!

A line of elephants, Jan Caspar Philips, 1727

LESSONS IN BEING HUMAN

Some animals can be trained to do quite complex jobs, and work alongside humans. Pets can be house-trained, and parrots can say words. The most amazing example, though, is a bonobo, or pygmy chimpanzee, named Kanzi. He grew up in captivity and has learned many human skills. He can recognise over 200 words, and use them by pointing to symbols for each word. He can also make a fire, play video games, chip at stones to make tools, and do basic cooking!

A dog learning to surf

As far as we know, humans are the most intelligent animals. Animals that are closely related to us, like chimpanzees, are also pretty smart and have big brains. But there are several other species that score highly in intelligence tests, and can do things like working out solutions to puzzles, or making and using tools. They include octopuses, crows, dolphins and orcas, elephants, dogs, squirrels and pigs.

SMARTY PANTS!

Two stuffed squirrels, touché!, Walter Potter, c. 1880

CAN ANIMALS INVENT THINGS?

Animals have been seen inventing new ways of doing things. In Japan, a macaque (a kind of monkey) began dipping her wild potatoes in the sea, as the salty water made them taste nicer. All the others copied her! One group of dolphins invented a way to protect their snouts from sharp coral while hunting, by holding sea sponges in their beaks. And some crows have figured out how to drop breadcrumbs into water to attract fish, which they then catch and eat.

A macaque washing a potato

GLOSSARY

Asteroid a rocky space object that orbits around the sun.

Bacteria a group of tiny, single-celled living things.

Bioluminescence light given off by living things, such as insects, fish or squid.

Calories units used to measure energy, especially the amount of energy in food.

Camouflage patterns or colouring that help a living thing to hide by matching its surroundings.

Carnivore an animal that feeds on other animals.

Domestication taming and breeding animals in order to keep them as pets or farm animals.

Echolocation detecting objects and surroundings by making a sound and listening to the echoes that bounce back. Bats and dolphins both use echolocation.

Ecosystem a habitat and the living things that live in it. The creatures in an ecosystem interact and depend on each other for survival.

Endangered at risk of dying out and becoming extinct. Many wild animals are now endangered.

Evolution a series of changes in living things that allow species to adapt to their surroundings, and new species to develop.

Extinct no longer existing. When a species is extinct, no members of that species are left alive.

Food chain a sequence of living things in which each one is eaten by the next one in the chain.

Gills breathing organs found in fish and some amphibians. They work by extracting oxygen from water.

Habitat the natural home or surroundings of a living thing. Animals are well-suited to surviving in their natural habitats.

Herbivore an animal that feeds on plants.

Hibernate to spend the winter in a sleep-like state to save on energy. Some hibernating animals do not eat for several months.

Instinct an automatic behaviour in an animal, which they do not have to be taught. For example, many birds have an instinct to build a nest for their eggs.

Invertebrate an animal that does not have a backbone, such as a worm, octopus or insect.

Keratin a substance found in many animals' bodies. It is used to grow body parts like hair, fingernails, claws, feathers, hooves and horns.

Mineral a pure, non-living substance found in nature, such as iron, diamond, salt or quartz.

Nectar a sweet liquid made inside flowers to attract insects.

Niche a particular role or way of surviving within an ecosystem. Each animal species evolves to fill a niche.

Nocturnal active mainly at night. Nocturnal animals rest or sleep during the day.

Omnivore an animal that feeds on a variety of food, including plants and other animals.

Oxygen a gas found in the air, which animals need to breathe in order to survive. Animals' body cells use oxygen to help them turn food into energy.

Paralyse To make a living thing unable to move its body.

Plankton A mixture of many types of tiny plants and animals that drift around in water. Plankton often provide food for water animals such as fish and whales.

Predator An animal that hunts and eats other animals.

Prehistoric From the time before history was first recorded. Prehistoric animals include dinosaurs and sabre-toothed tigers.

Prey An animal that is hunted and eaten by another animal.

Regurgitate To bring swallowed food back up into the mouth. Some animals do this to feed their young.

Retina A layer of cells inside an eyeball that can detect light and send information to the brain.

Selective breeding Selecting particular living things for their useful qualities and breeding them (helping them to have young). Farmers do this in order to make wild species more suitable for farming.

Species An individual type of living thing. Animals of the same species can breed and have young that also belong to that species.

Venom A poisonous or painful substance that an animal injects into its prey or into an enemy, for example by biting or stinging. Many snakes, spiders and scorpions are venomous.

Vertebrate An animal that has a backbone, such as a fish, bird or human.

Water vapour Water in the form of a gas. It is found in the air, and in the breath that animals breathe out.

INDEX

ILLUSTRATION CREDITS

6-7 Shutterstock 6 ©Corey A. Ford/Dreamstime.com
7b USO/iStock 9 CSIRO 10 Ploucquet of Stuttgart
from a daguerreotype by Claudet 11a fototrav/
iStock 11b Drawing Dave Bezzina 13 Dopeyden/
istock 14 Biosphoto/Claudius Thiriet/Diomedia 15a
Biosphoto/Roger Eritja/Diomedia 15b mashuk/iStock
17 Rijksmuseum Museum, Amsterdam 18a ©FLPA/S
& D & K Maslow/age fotostock 18b ©Mc Donald
Wildlife Ph/age fotostock 19a Rijksmuseum Museum,
Amsterdam 19b Clare Havill/Alamy Stock Photo
21 DeAgostini/Diomedia 22 alice-photo/iStock
23a imageBROKER/REX/Shutterstock 23b
imageBROKER/REX/Shutterstock 26 Rijksmuseum
Museum, Amsterdam 27a Drawing Dave Bezzina
27b koi88/iStock 29 ©David Jenkins/age fotostock
30a Ben Cooper/Superstock 30b paulafrench/iStock
31 © Victoria and Albert Museum, London 33
Shutterstock 34 Universal images group/Superstock
35a Wellcome Library, London 35b Ingram publishing/
Diomedia 37 Shutterstock 39b Wellcome Library,
London 38 Bill Curtsinger/National Geographic
Creative 40-41 Mark Deeble and Victoria Stone/Getty
images 42a Rijksmuseum Museum, Amsterdam
43 axelbueckert/iStock 44-45 Avalon/Picture Nature/
Alamy Stock Photo 46 imageBROKER RM/Norbert
Probst/Diomedia 47a Pete Oxford/Minden Pictures/
Getty images 47b Biosphoto/Michel Gunther/Diomedia
48-49 DeAgostini/Diomedia 50a Photograph Leonard
Lee Rue III 50b UIG Education/Encyclopaedia
Britannica/Diomedia 51 Biosphoto/Jeffrey Rotman/

Diomedia 53 Wellcome Library, London 54-55
Shutterstock 54a Rijksmuseum Museum, Amsterdam
54b wasantistock/iStock 55 Rijksmuseum Museum,
Amsterdam 57 kuri2341/iStock 59a Andrew_Howe/
iStock 59b Rijksmuseum Museum, Amsterdam
58 blickwinkel/Alamy Stock Photo 61 Richard
Ellis/Getty images 62-63 NASA 63a Superstock
RM/Diomedia 63b SuperStock RM/SCUBAZOO/
Diomedia 65 bazilfoto/iStock 66 FourOaks/iStock
67a Rijksmuseum Museum, Amsterdam 67b Paulo
Oliveira/Alamy Stock Photo 70a Life on White/Getty
images 70b Design Pics Inc/REX/Shutterstock
71 Wellcome Library, London 73 Red Circle Images/
Diomedia 74a Kazushi_Inagaki/iStock 74b George
Arents Collection, The New York Public Library
75 Specialist Stock RM/Michael Nolan/Diomedia
76-77 British Library London UK/Diomedia 78a
LOOK/Konrad Wothe 78b Picture Library/REX/
Shutterstock 79 duncan1890/iStock 80-81
Shutterstock 81 Heritage Images/Fine Art Images/
Diomedia 82a SuperStock RF/Stock Connection/
Diomedia 82b Stephen Dalton/Minden Pictures/
Getty images 83 Wellcome Library, London 86a
David Tipling Photo Library/Alamy Stock Photo
86b LatitudeStock/Alamy Stock Photo 87 Cultura
RM/Alamy Stock Photo 89 Cincinnati Art Museum,
Ohio, USA,Gift of Mr & Mrs Charles Fleischmann in
memory of JuliusFleischmann/Bridgeman Images
90a Zuma press/Diomedia 91 Cyril Ruoso/Minden
Pictures/Getty images

First published in the United Kingdom in 2017
by Thames & Hudson Ltd, 181A High Holborn,
London WC1V 7QX

Why don't fish drown? © 2017 Thames & Hudson
Ltd, London
Original illustrations © 2017 Claire Goble

Text by Anna Claybourne
Designed by Anna Perotti at By The Sky Design

British Library Cataloguing-in-Publication Data
A catalogue record for this book is available
from the British Library

ISBN 978-0-500-65126-1

Manufactured in China by Imago

To find out about all our publications, please visit
www.thamesandhudson.com.
There you can subscribe to our e-newsletter, browse or download
our current catalogue, and buy any titles that are in print.

THE OLYMPICS

MODERN OLYMPIC GAMES

REVISED AND UPDATED

Haydn Middleton

Heinemann
LIBRARY

www.heinemann.co.uk/library
Visit our website to find out more information about Heinemann Library books.

To order:
☎ Phone 44 (0) 1865 888066
▤ Send a fax to 44 (0)1865 314091
▭ Visit the Heinemann Library Bookshop at www.heinemann.co.uk/library to browse our catalogue and order online.

First published in Great Britain by Heinemann Library, Halley Court, Jordan Hill, Oxford OX2 8EJ, part of Harcourt Education.
Heinemann Library is a registered trademark of Harcourt Education Ltd.

Editorial: Joanna Talbot
Design: Philippa Jenkins
Picture Research: Tracy Cummins
Production: Alison Parsons

Originated by Modern Age Repro
Printed and bound by Leo Paper Group

ISBN 978 0 431 19160 7
12 11 10 09 08
10 9 8 7 6 5 4 3 2 1

British Library Cataloguing in Publication Data
Middleton, Haydn
   Modern olympic games. – (The olympics)
   1. Olympic Games – Juvenile literature
   2. Olympics – Records – Juvenile literature
   I. Title.
   796.4·8

A full catalogue record for this book is available from the British Library.

Acknowledgements
The publishers would like to thank the following for permission to reproduce photographs: Allsport: pp. **6, 7, 8, 9, 11** (left), **12, 14, 17, 18, 19, 20, 22, 24, 25**; Colorsport: pp. **11** (right), **23, 28, 29**; Corbis: pp. **15** (ZUMA/Axel), **16** (Nik Wheeler); **26** (ZUMA/K.C. Alfred), **27** (epa/GIGI ARCAINI); Michael Holford: p. **5**; REUTERS p. **4** (Clive Rose/Pool); Redux: p. **13** (The New York Times/Doug Mills).

Cover photograph reproduced with permission of AP Photo/Lionel Cironneau.

The publishers would like to thank John Townsend for his assistance with the preparation of this book.

Every effort has been made to contact copyright holders of any material reproduced in this book. Any omissions will be rectified in subsequent printings if notice is given to the publishers.

CONTENTS

Any words appearing in the text in bold, **like this**, are explained in the Glossary.

INTRODUCTION

The Olympic Games are by far the most important international athletic competition in the world. Every four years they bring together thousands of the world's best athletes. Millions of people have been able to attend the Games and experience the amazing atmosphere for themselves. Billions of people all over the world now watch the Games on television (up to 4 billion viewers!). But just 100 years ago, no one would ever have imagined how the Games would develop. The Olympic Games of the 21st century are nothing like the first modern Olympics that began in 1896.

Since 1924 there have been separate Winter Olympics that take place every four years. They, too, have been steadily growing for more than 80 years.

A record 2,508 athletes (960 women and 1,548 men) from 80 countries competed in the 84 events at the Turin Winter Games in Italy, 2006. There were 18,000 volunteer helpers to make the Games run smoothly. ▼

Over the years, people have posed many questions about the Olympic Games. How much longer can the Olympic Games keep going? Are they getting too big to organise? Are they getting too expensive to run? Although the Games had to stop during two world wars, they look set to continue for years to come, as they just keep getting bigger and better!

OLYMPIC ORIGINS

Although the modern Games began in 1896, they were not the first Olympics ever. For those, you have to go back almost 3,000 years – to ancient Greece. The five-day-long Games held then featured running, combat sports, the **pentathlon**, horse-riding, and chariot races.

We have records of winners dating back to 776BC but the ancient Games came to an end in AD393, when the Roman Emperor, Theodosius I, banned all non-Christian worship throughout his empire. Since the Olympics were held in honour of the Greek gods, they had to come to an end as well. But just over 1,500 years later, they began again in their modern form. Turn over and find out how it happened.

This ancient Greek vase painting shows the old Greek sport of *pankration* – man-to-man combat in which almost any form of **aggression** was allowed. ▼

BRING BACK THE GAMES!

The Games did not start again of their own accord. By the end of the 19th century, plenty of people in Europe and America were keen on sport. Some might even have dreamed of a brand new global Games, based on the ancient Greek Olympics. But one man above all others made this dream come true. His name was Pierre de Frédy, Baron de Coubertin, a French **aristocrat** who was an active sportsman himself!

A RELIGION OF SPORT

De Coubertin (1863–1937) was a widely travelled man. In Britain he saw how important sport was in the **public schools**. In the USA he admired the highly developed training and coaching programmes at the colleges. Sport became a kind of religion to him.

Baron Pierre de Coubertin, father of the modern Olympic Games.

Through sport, he believed, 'our body rises above its animal nature'. Sporting contests were 'the means of bringing to perfection the strong and hopeful youth … helping towards the perfection of all human society'. 'Sport,' he concluded, 'should allow man to know himself, to control himself, and to conquer himself.' (Only man, you will notice, not woman. Like the ancient Greeks, and most other people of his own time, de Coubertin thought a woman's place was in the home, not the stadium.)

From 1892, he set about trying to convert others to his strong faith in sport. His aim was to set up some Games where the 'youth of the world' could come together in peaceful, character-building competition: a modern Olympics. It was especially important to him that everyone taking part should be **amateur**. The glory of being an Olympian, not money, would be the athletes' reward.

BIRTH OF AN 'OLYMPIC FAMILY'

It might seem surprising now, but at first de Coubertin found little support for his grand idea. Then in June 1894, at a congress in Paris, he persuaded **delegates** from twelve countries to back his plan to revive the Olympics. The Games would be held in Athens, the capital of Greece, in 1896. Then, at four-yearly intervals, they would be hosted by other major cities. Soon more countries came into this new 'Olympic family', and an International Olympic Committee (IOC) was set up to organise and oversee the Games. De Coubertin himself was president of the IOC for 30 years.

The first modern Olympic Games were duly held in Athens over ten days in June 1896. An estimated 245 men – from Greece, Germany, France and Great Britain – took part in 43 events. Few of the performances were brilliant. In fact, in events like the discus and long jump, champions from ancient times may well have achieved greater distances! But the Games were hugely popular with the big crowds that came to watch. The world's appetite had been whetted.

This was the official report of the 1896 Games. Athletes from fourteen different nations took part.

The Olympic Charter states that 'the Olympic Games are competitions between athletes in individual or team events and not between countries.' But ever since 1896, nations have competed against one another for the most sporting success. ▶

7

THE GAMES ROLL ON: 1900–1936

YEAR	WHERE	WHEN	COMPETITORS		NATIONS	EVENTS
			Men	Women		
1900	Paris, France	14 May–28 Oct	1206	19	26	88
1904	St. Louis, USA	1 July–23 Nov	681	6	13	89
1908	London, England	27 Apr–31 Oct	1,999	36	22	109
1912	Stockholm, Sweden	5 May–22 July	2,490	57	28	102
1916	Berlin, Germany	Cancelled due to WW1				
1920	Antwerp, Belgium	20 Apr–12 Sept	2,591	78	29	154
1924	Paris, France	4 May–27 July	2,956	136	44	126
1928	Amsterdam, Netherlands	17 May–12 Aug	2,724	290	46	109
1932	Los Angeles, USA	30 July–14 Aug	1,281	127	37	117
1936	Berlin, Germany	1 Aug–16 Aug	3,738	328	49	129

The official Olympic poster advertising the 1912 Games – the first at which nations from five continents (North and South America, Asia, Australia, and Europe) took part.

OLYMPIC GAMES
STOCKHOLM 1912
JUNE 29 th – JULY 22 nd.

The table above shows how the Olympic story continued in the 40 years after 1896. As time went on, the Games were organised over a shorter and shorter period. For the earlier Games, the word 'disorganised' was closer to the truth. Some competitors were not even aware that the event they were taking part in was part of the Olympic Games. Sometimes, too, **professional** sportsmen were allowed to compete.

Slowly but surely organisation improved, and there were fewer disputes over which events were official and which were not. The fifth Games at Stockholm set a new standard for efficiency – but then the 1916 Games never took place, because of World War One. In ancient Greece this would not have happened. Back then, a **truce** would have been declared – to let the athletes travel to the Games and compete in safety.

► The men's 4x400 m relay at the Berlin Olympics of 1936 – the first to be shown on television. Berliners could watch the Games for free on giant screens in the city's theatres.

GAMES BETWEEN THE WARS

The Olympics resumed in 1920. The Games were held in Belgium, which had suffered horribly during World War One. 'All this is quite nice,' remarked the Belgian king at the opening ceremony, 'but it certainly lacks people.' The 1924 Games in Paris had bigger crowds, but trouble kept breaking out because the fans were so aggressive in their support – definitely not in the 'Olympic spirit'.

Women participated in **track-and-field** events for the first time at the 1928 Games in Amsterdam. Before then they had taken part in tennis, swimming, golf, archery, figure skating, yachting, and fencing. At the next Games, in Los Angeles, fewer women *and* men competed. This was partly because it was too expensive for many Europeans to travel to the faraway USA. At that time, making and selling alcohol was against American law. But the athletes from France and Italy were allowed to drink wine – because they said it was a vital part of their diet!

In 1931 the International Olympic Committee decided to stage the eleventh Games in Germany. Two years later Hitler and his **Nazi** Party came to power. Despite much protest, the 1936 Games went ahead in Berlin. As a spectacle they were lavish, since Hitler wanted to prove to the world the 'supremacy' (total superiority) of the German people. Again, this was far from the true Olympic spirit. Hitler's influence over the Olympic story extended beyond 1936, when World War Two led to a cancellation of the Games until 1948.

TRULY GLOBAL OLYMPICS: 1948-1996

In the 50 years after World War Two, the Olympics steadily grew. More and more competitors took part, more countries got involved and more events were added. This table clearly shows the rate of growth.

YEAR	WHERE	WHEN	COMPETITORS		NATIONS	EVENTS
			Men	Women		
1940 and 1944	–	Cancelled due to WWII				
1948	London, England	29 July–14 Aug	3,714	385	59	136
1952	Helsinki, Finland	19 July–3 Aug	4,407	518	69	149
1956	Melbourne, Australia	22 Nov–8 Dec	2,813	371	72	151
1960	Rome, Italy	25 Aug–11 Sept	4,738	610	83	150
1964	Tokyo, Japan	10 Oct–24 Oct	4,457	683	93	163
1968	Mexico City, Mexico	12 Oct–27 Oct	4,750	781	112	172
1972	Munich, West Germany	26 Aug–10 Sep	6,065	1,058	121	195
1976	Montreal, Canada	17 July–1 Aug	4,781	1,247	92	198
1980	Moscow, USSR	19 July–3 Aug	4.092	1,125	80	203
1984	Los Angeles, USA	28 July–12 Aug	5,230	1,567	140	221
1988	Seoul, South Korea	17 Sept–2 Oct	6,279	2,186	159	237
1992	Barcelona, Spain	24 July–9 Aug	6,636	2,708	169	257
1996	Atlanta, USA	19 July–4 Aug	6,797	3,513	197	271

◄ For the first time ever, the Olympics went to Asia for the spectacular 1964 Games in Tokyo.

WAR AND PATCHY PEACE

Germany and Japan, which were defeated in World War Two, were not invited to London's 1948 Games. It took time for the rifts to mend.

There was also friction between countries during the **Cold War** of the 1950s and 1960s when **Communist** countries like the USSR and non-communist countries like the United States were bitter rivals. They saw the Games as a way to prove their governments were superior, which was far from the spirit intended for the Olympics.

The last Summer Games of the 20th century were in Atlanta, USA, in 1996. The ex-Olympic champion boxer Muhammad Ali lit the Olympic flame. ▶

PEACE AT LAST

There were all kinds of rows between countries in the second half of the 20th century, resulting in some **boycotting** the Games altogether as a form of protest. The International Olympic Committee (IOC) banned South Africa from taking part for 28 years, because of its brutal **apartheid** system.

The chart opposite shows that only 80 countries took part in the Moscow Olympics of 1980. That was because 65 countries kept away to protest at the USSR's invasion of Afghanistan the year before.

By the 1990s, political problems between countries had calmed down so that by 1996 a record 197 nations took part. But that number was to grow even more in the new **millennium**.

THE 21ST CENTURY

The first Olympic Games of the new **millennium** were held in Sydney, Australia in the summer of 2000. A total of 10,651 athletes (4,069 women and 6,582 men) competed in 300 events, making them larger than any previous Games. They were also special for the British rower Steven Redgrave, who became the first rower to win gold medals at five consecutive Olympics.

NEW RECORDS

The number of women competitors has kept growing in the 21st century. In 2002, the Olympic Winter Games in Salt Lake City, USA, included the women's bobsleigh for the first time. The winner was Vonetta Flowers, of the United States, who became the first black athlete to earn a winter gold.

In 2004 the Olympic Games returned to Greece, the home of both the ancient Olympics and the first modern Olympics. With more events than ever, the Games now included women's wrestling. Women's **sabre** fencing also appeared for the first time. Mariel Zagunis of the United States won the gold medal. It was the first United States victory in fencing.

Despite the war in Iraq, the football team from Iraq qualified for the Olympic tournament and made it to the semi-finals. This was another of the highlights of the 2004 Games.

◄ The Olympic Stadium in Sydney, Australia, was the centrepiece of the 27th Games in 2000.

▲ The Beijing National Stadium in China, also known as the 'bird's nest', is the main track and field stadium for the 2008 Summer Olympics.

WHERE NEXT?

For the first time ever, it became China's turn to host the Olympic Games, for 2008 in the new impressive Beijing Stadium. After that, the 2010 Winter Olympics will return to Canada (Vancouver). The 30th Olympic Games return to London for the third time in 2012, when the organisers hope the Games will be bigger and better than ever before.

FUTURE GAMES

Just where will the Olympic Games be held in 2016? More than 20 cities around the world are already hoping they could be in with a chance of hosting the Games. The winner will be announced at the end of 2009. Already some cities have expressed interest in hosting the 2020 Olympics! Some of those making a bid are:

Chicago, USA

Tokyo, Japan

Prague, Czech Republic

Rio de Janeiro, Brazil

WHO GETS THE GAMES?

PRESIDENTS OF THE INTERNATIONAL OLYMPIC COMMITTEE

1894–96	Demetrius Vikelas (Greece)
1896–1925	Baron Pierre de Coubertin (France)
1925–42	Count Henri de Baillet-Latour (Belgium)
1946–52	J Sigfrid Edström (Sweden)
1952–72	Avery Brundage (USA)
1972–80	Lord Killanin (Ireland)
1980–2001	Juan Antonio Samaranch (Spain)
2001–	Jacques Rogge (Belgium)

Besides the organisation required, it has also been a very complicated and increasingly expensive business to stage the Olympic Games. Greece, the host country of the first modern Games in 1896, wanted them to be staged there permanently. This suggestion was made again in the 1980s, since the cost of organising each new Games had become so huge for the cities involved.

Both times, the International Olympic Committee (IOC) said no: the Olympic Games are truly international, and should therefore be staged all over the world. An added attraction of this is that a Games held in, say, Tokyo has a very different feel and flavour to one held in Mexico City.

THE OLYMPIC CHARTER

The Olympic Charter is the official set of rules for the Olympic Movement. It says that some of the IOC's aims are: 'to encourage the organisation and development of sports and sports competitions; ... to fight against any form of discrimination affecting the Olympic Movement; to lead the fight against doping in sport ... and to see to it that the Olympic Games are held in conditions which demonstrate a responsible concern for environmental issues.'

In 1993 these delegates from Sydney, Australia, celebrated their winning bid to stage the 2000 Olympics in their home city.

BEST BIDDER WINS

In July 2001 in Moscow, Beijing was elected the host city for the Games. It was agreed that 'a Beijing Games would leave a unique legacy to China and to sports. The Commission is confident that Beijing could organise an excellent Games.'

In July 2005, London finally won a two-way fight with Paris by 54 votes to 50 to host the 2012 Games. Bids from Moscow, New York, and Madrid had already been eliminated. London celebrated the news, even though some Londoners thought the Games would cost a fortune and cause chaos!

In 2007, a survey showed how hosting the Games would bring much money into the country. The survey asked questions of people from 35 countries around the world. Of those who said they wanted to visit the UK, one in three said the Games were their main reason for coming. Visitors who come for sporting events are likely to spend almost twice as long in a country as other tourists and are likely to be younger.

News of London's victory delighted flag-waving supporters who had gathered in Trafalgar Square.

GLOBAL VILLAGE

◀ Part of the Olympic village for the 1996 Games in Atlanta, USA. The organisers of these Olympics called them 'the largest, peacetime social event in human history'.

To ensure the London bid was successful, the team promised that every competitor at the 2012 Olympic Games and Paralympic Games would have a bed in a state-of-the-art Olympic Village. That's well over 17,000 beds! After the games, the 'village' where everyone will stay is planned to become a district of Stratford City, a multi-billion pound development project on the former railway goods yard near the Olympic Park.

VILLAGE OR MINI-CITY?

At the earliest modern Games, athletes and officials made do with whatever quarters they could find. The American team of 1912 just stayed on board the liner that had brought them across the ocean to Stockholm. Competitors in Antwerp in 1920 lived in the city's schools – sleeping eight to a classroom!

But at the Los Angeles Games of 1932, the first special Olympic village was built. It was more like a mini-city with its own post office, hospital, fire station, and security guards. The guards had instructions to admit no women. There were only 127 female competitors and they all stayed in a Los Angeles hotel. A village was also built for the Berlin Games of 1936, and at Helsinki in 1952 there were two – because the **USSR**-led **Communist** countries demanded separate secure quarters for their competitors, partly for fear that they might **defect** to the West.

The building of more recent Olympic villages has helped make host cities better places for their own citizens to live in. In order to erect a village for the Barcelona Games of 1992, a whole stretch of the waterfront was **reclaimed** and developed. Then, after the Games, local people moved into the specially built low-rise apartments and made them their homes.

VILLAGE LIFE

Judo silver-medallist Nicola Fairbrother lived in the Olympic village at Barcelona in 1992. 'You can taste the apprehension in the air,' she wrote afterwards, 'sense the hopes and the dreams. All the food in the village was free. You could eat when, and as much as, you liked. Soon the main food hall became like a magnet for socialising.

'I also have vivid memories of the atmosphere walking about the village. It was like a bond that existed through every competitor in the village, regardless of colour, size, shape or sport. You could watch African runners lope by, followed by a group of tiny, Hungarian gymnasts and the Chinese volleyball team and there would be the same look in all of their faces. Everyone in the village seemed united by the incredible experience, everyone seemed alive.'

By 1992 **professional** players were allowed to take part in many Olympic events. The USA's basketball 'Dream Team' led by 'Magic' Johnson at the Barcelona Games contained eleven multi-millionaires. Being such superstars, they bypassed the Olympic village and stayed in $900-a-night hotel suites elsewhere in Barcelona. Not quite in the true Olympic spirit?

THE MARATHON: ANCIENT MEETS MODERN

The longest Olympic race is the marathon. It has been a highlight of the men's programme of events in all the modern Games, and since 1984 there has been a women's marathon too. The idea for the race came from an old Greek legend. In 490BC the Greeks won a famous victory over the Persians at the Battle of Marathon. It was said that Pheidipiddes, a **professional** runner, then rushed the enormous distance of about 40 kilometres back to Athens to break the good news. 'Be joyful, we win!' he declared on arriving – and then dropped dead of exhaustion. Whether the story was true or not, the organisers of the 1896 Games in Athens decided to hold a long-distance race named after the great battle.

LOCAL HERO

The first Olympic marathon was 40 kilometres (25 miles) long. Although it was run mainly on roads outside Athens, it was due to finish in the Olympic stadium. To the joy of the huge crowd waiting there, the first man home was local farmer Spiridon Louis, in a time of 2 hours 58 minutes 50 seconds. It was Greece's only victory at the Games and local merchants tried to shower Louis with gifts. All he accepted was a horse and cart to transport water to his village.

◄ Spiridon Louis, the first Olympic marathon winner in 1896. Forty years later, the German Olympic Organising Committee brought him to Berlin for the 1936 Games. There he presented to German leader Adolf Hitler a laurel **wreath** from the sacred grove at Olympia, the site of the ancient Olympics. He died in 1940.

MEMORABLE MARATHON MOMENTS

The marathon has rarely been short of drama. In 1904 at St Louis, Zulu tribesman Lentauw (one of the first two black Africans to compete in the Olympics) was chased off the course and through a cornfield by dogs. He still finished ninth.

The 1908 London marathon began at Windsor Castle and ended in the Olympic stadium at Shepherd's Bush – a distance of 42 kilometres (26 miles). The runners then had to push themselves through another 352 metres (385 yards) around the track – so that the finishing line would be right in front of Queen Alexandra's **royal box**! But in all but two of the Games since then, the official marathon distance has been set at 26 miles 385 yards (or about 42 kilometres).

In 1960 Rome staged a night marathon, since the daytime heat was just too great. Both that race and the 1964 marathon were won by Ethiopian Abebe Bikila.

In Barcelona in 1992, Mongolian Pyambuu Tuul recorded a time of 4 hours and 44 seconds – the slowest in 84 years. But Tuul had been blinded by an explosion in 1978, then in 1990 he had run in the New York marathon with a guide's help. A year later an operation gave him partial sight, so he entered for the Barcelona Olympics – not to win but 'to show that a man has many possibilities'.

The 2004 Athens marathon followed the same route as the 1896 race, beginning in Marathon and ending in Athens' Panathenaic Stadium. In the men's race, Vanderlei de Lima of Brazil was in the lead with less than 7 kilometres (4 miles) to go when a man pushed him off the course. De Lima still managed to go on to win the bronze medal and was awarded the Pierre de Coubertin Medal because of his true Olympic spirit.

▲ The winner of the third-ever women's marathon, at Barcelona in 1992, was Russia's Valentina Yegorova. Hundreds of friends and neighbours back in her farming village of Iziderkino bought a 30-year-old TV set and crowded around it in the street to watch her take the gold.

WHICH SPORTS?

How many different Olympic sports can you name? Most people think of athletics, swimming, and gymnastics because these sports attract more media coverage than most. But there are many more. In fact, the 2008 Olympics includes 28 sports. That's 302 events in total – one more than in Athens in 2004. There are 165 men's events, 127 women's events, and 10 mixed events. Nine new events will be held, including BMX cycling, steeplechase for women, 10 kilometres (6.2 miles) swimming for men and women, and team events in table tennis.

OLYMPIC SPORTS FEATURED IN BEIJING, CHINA, 2008

Aquatics (diving, swimming, synchronized swimming, and water polo)

Archery

Athletics

Badminton

Baseball

Basketball

Boxing

Canoeing

Cycling

Equestrianism

Fencing

Football

Gymnastics

Handball

Hockey

Judo

Modern Pentathlon

Rowing

Sailing

Shooting

Softball

Table tennis

Tai kwon do

Tennis

Triathlon

Volleyball

Weightlifting

Wrestling

▲ Canoeing: a fiercely contested Olympic sport. Kayak events feature paddles with a blade at each end. The paddles in Canadian canoeing have only one blade.

The International Olympic Committee's Programme Commission constantly discusses Olympic sports which already take place, and possible new ones for the future. At various Games since 1896, many sports have tried and failed to find a permanent place in the Olympics. The list below shows some of the sports that now belong in the mist of Olympic history.

DISCONTINUED OLYMPIC SPORTS

(Years in brackets show when they were staged)

Cricket (1900) Britain won – beating a French team made up mostly of Englishmen!

Croquet (1900) France won all three croquet events.

Golf (1900, 1904) In 1904 Canadian joker George Lyon became Olympic champion – and accepted a silver trophy after walking down the path to the ceremony on his hands.

Jeu de Paume – 'Real Tennis' (1908) American Jay Gould won gold.

Lacrosse (1904, 1908) In 1908, when Frank Dixon of Canada broke his stick, British opponent R. G. W. Martin offered to withdraw from the game until a new one was found. The Canadians went on to win the Olympic final.

Motorboating (1908) Briton Thomas Thornycroft won gold in two different classes. Forty-four years later, aged 70, he was selected for the British yachting team at the 1952 Helsinki Games.

Polo (1900, 1908, 1920, 1924, 1936) In the last competition, Argentina won gold in front of a crowd of 45,000 people.

Racquets (1908) Britain won a clean sweep of all the medals.

Roque – hard-surface croquet (1904) A clean sweep for the USA.

Rugby union (1900, 1908, 1920, 1924) Team-member Daniel Carroll won gold for Australia in 1908 and then for the USA in 1920. No one else has ever won gold medals for representing different countries.

Tug-of-war (1900, 1904, 1908, 1912, 1920) The first team to pull the other for six feet (1.8 metres) was declared the winner. In 1908 teams of British policemen came first, second, and third.

Art (1912–1948) Until 1948, medals were awarded for works of art inspired by sport. The medals were divided into five categories: architecture, literature, music, painting, and sculpture.

OLYMPIC TRADITIONS

Processions and parades took place at the ancient Greek Games and now they are dramatic features of the modern Olympics. Each new opening ceremony – watched by enormous TV audiences – seems to outdo the last for spectacular entertainments and effects. The procession of competitors is still led by Greece, followed by all the other national teams in alphabetical order, with the host country's team appearing last. In Melbourne in 1956, a seventeen-year-old Chinese boy suggested that everyone should walk together as a single **multicultural** nation at the Games' closing ceremony – it made a wonderful sight.

THE OLYMPIC OATH

'In the name of all competitors, I promise that we will take part in these Olympic Games, respecting and abiding by the rules which govern them, committing ourselves to a sport without doping and without drugs, in the true spirit of sportsmanship, for the glory of sport and the honour of our teams.'

Since 1920, a representative of the host country has taken this oath at the opening ceremony of each Games. Usually the oath-taker is a veteran of previous Games.

MASCOTS

The first Olympic mascot made its appearance at the 1968 Winter Games in Grenoble – a cartoon-like character on skis, called Schuss. Since then each Games has had its own named mascot – usually chosen because of a connection with the host country. Popular mascots have included Misha the Bear at Moscow in 1980, Waldi the Dachshund at Munich in 1972, and Cobi the Dog at Barcelona in 1992. Since 1980 the Winter Games have also had mascots.

◀ At Barcelona, Spain, in 1992, a crowd of 100,000 people and a TV audience of two billion watched one of the most breathtaking opening ceremonies ever.

TENDING THE FLAME

At Amsterdam in 1928 the Olympic flame was first lit, and it burned throughout the Games. Eight years later, the first 'torch relay' was run. More than 3,000 runners brought the 'sacred fire' from Olympia, where the sun's rays ignited it, to Berlin more than 3,000 kilometres (1,864 miles) away. In 1952, for the Helsinki Games, the torch first travelled by air. Twenty-four years later, the flame's energy sent a laser beam from Greece to Montreal – and lit an identical torch! Then in 1996, there was a moving moment when ex-Olympic champion boxer Muhammad Ali, suffering from **Parkinson's disease**, lit the Olympic flame in Atlanta, in his own country.

Since 1920 this has been the official Olympic flag. It was designed by the founder of the modern Games, Baron de Coubertin. The coloured rings are nowadays believed to represent the five inhabited continents of the world, linked together by sport. These five colours were chosen because, in 1920, at least one of them appeared in the flag of each participating country. ▼

MEDAL CEREMONIES

In ancient Greece, all the Olympic winners were presented with olive **wreaths** at the end of the Games. At each modern Games until 1928, victors' medals were also given out at the closing ceremony. Now medals are presented to the winners of each event as it takes place. (Incidentally, Olympic gold medals are 92.5 per cent solid silver, with 6 grams of gold on top.)

The podium or victory stand – with its 1-2-3 positions – was introduced in 1932. Some people think **national anthems** should not be played at Olympic medal presentations. After all, the Games are meant to be international. At Tokyo in 1964, when Abebe Bikila received a gold medal for Ethiopia, the Japanese band did not know the Ethiopian anthem – so it played Japan's anthem instead!

MEN ONLY?

In ancient times very few women were allowed to watch Olympic events. No women at all were allowed to take part in them. When the modern Games began in 1896, there were still no women competitors. Many people believed that women's bodies could not cope with the demands of top-level sport. Some thought, too, that a woman's true place was in the home, not the stadium.

In the 100 years since the start of the Modern Games in 1896, the number of competitors rose from just 245 men to 6,797, as well as 3,513 women. The gap between the number of male and female athletes is closing all the time. Within the next 20 years, will the number of women even overtake the number of men?

WOMEN ADMITTED AT LAST

The earliest female Olympians were golfers and tennis players. American Margaret Abbott won a golfing gold medal at a Paris tournament in 1900, without even realising that she was taking part in the Olympic Games!

The first Olympic marathon for women was staged in Los Angeles in 1984. It was won by American Joan Benoit (pictured wearing a hat) in a time of 2 hrs 24 mins 52 secs. That was quite an improvement on the first official, pre-Olympic time clocked by a female marathon runner – 3 hrs 40 mins 22 secs by Violet Piercy of Great Britain in 1926. (Even so, Piercy's record stood unchallenged for 37 years!)

COLLAPSE

In 1928, six of the eight entrants in the women's 800-metre race were said to have collapsed at the finish line in an 'exhausted state'. Poor training methods and the Amsterdam heat were two major causes of distress. That event was cancelled until 1960.

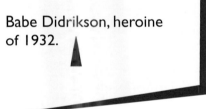

Babe Didrikson, heroine of 1932.

Women made their debut in Olympic athletics events at Amsterdam in 1928. For the first time women competed in the 100-metre run, the 4 × 100-metre relay, the 800-metre run, the discus, and the high jump. It was not until 1984 that women were allowed to compete in the most gruelling Olympic race of all – the marathon.

A WOMAN CALLED BABE

One woman who did more than most for the cause of female Olympians was Mildred 'Babe' Didrikson. At the Los Angeles Games in 1932, this confident eighteen-year-old American announced: 'I came out here to beat everybody in sight, and that is exactly what I'm going to do.' She proceeded to win the javelin and broke the world record to win the 80-metre hurdles. In the high jump, she tied for first place and claimed another world record, but received only a silver medal because an official had called her head-first 'diving' style illegal. She would doubtless have won more gold, but women then were allowed to compete in only three events – even though Babe had qualified for five. In later life she excelled in basketball and golf. Someone once asked if there was anything she did not play. 'Yeah,' she replied. 'Dolls.'

FOR THE LOVE OF SPORT

Amateurs are meant to play sports purely for the love of it. **Professionals** receive material rewards. Nowadays almost all Olympic competitors are professionals; even top soccer players are allowed to take part. Sporting standards are so high that few athletes could train to the right level and do regular jobs. Yet that was what the organisers of the first modern Games wanted them to do. And, until quite recent times, amateurism remained the Olympic ideal.

A NOBLE TRADITION

'The important thing in the Olympic Games is not winning but taking part. The essential thing in life is not conquering but fighting well.' Baron de Coubertin and his fellow-organisers of the first modern Games believed very strongly in this point of view. For them, simply taking part was its own reward. Certainly there was no question of money being paid – either as a prize for the winners of events, or to competitors as expenses for their training programmes. Olympic sport was thus a glorious hobby for those who could afford to take part.

But the line between amateur and professional in Olympic sport was never completely clear. Spiridon Louis won the first marathon in 1896, and received a simple laurel **wreath** for his achievement. But his fans also promised him a multitude of gifts, including free groceries, free travel, and free haircuts for life! 'Material rewards' like these did sometimes go to the victors.

Olympic athletes were once meant to be amateurs, but competing in sport these days can be expensive. Starting in the 1970s, the rules began to change, and athletes who trained full-time were allowed to be paid. Now many Olympic stars also receive money to **endorse** products. Snowboarder Shaun White of the USA had many **sponsorship** deals as well as his own clothing line, and that was before he won his gold medal!

PARALYMPIC PROGRESS

In the first part of the modern Olympic era, there was no place for athletes who were physically disabled. This seemed unfortunate to Sir Ludwig Guttman, who went on to become the founder of the Paralympics.

◀ In Turin in 2006, disabled athletes competed in five sports: wheelchair curling, Alpine skiing, ice sledge hockey, cross-country skiing, and biathlon. Vladimir Kiselev of Russia won the gold medal in the men's sitting 12.5-kilometre (7.8-mile) biathlon competition.

In 1948 Guttman was director of the National Spinal Injuries Centre at Stoke Mandeville Hospital, UK. His original idea was to hold competitive sports for people with spinal injuries at the Stoke Mandeville Games. Soon people with other disabilities and from other nations got involved, and in 1960 a four-yearly 'parallel Olympics' began. In that year 400 athletes from 23 countries competed in Rome. This had grown to 3,806 athletes from 136 countries competing in 19 sports in the 2004 Paralympics in Athens.

The Paralympic Games have always been held in the same year as the Olympic Games. Since the 1988 Seoul Summer Games and the 1992 Albertville Winter Games, they have also taken place at the same venues as the Olympic Games. From 2008 on, the Paralympics will always take place just after the Olympic Games, using the same sporting venues and facilities.

The Paralympics are now elite (highest-level) sport events for athletes from six different disability groups. They emphasise the participants' athletic achievements rather than their disability, and competition is as fierce as in the Olympics themselves.

ICE-COLD OLYMPICS

There was figure skating in the Olympic Games of 1908 and 1920, and ice hockey too was played in 1920. But in 1924 the International Olympic Committee established a completely separate Winter Olympic Games. From then including 1992, they were always staged in the same year as the Summer Games, although not always in the same country (see table, right). But beginning with the 1994 Games at Lillehammer, the Winter Olympics were rescheduled to take place in the even-numbered years that fell between the Summer Games.

In the 1924 Games at Chamonix, there were 14 events in five different sports. At Turin in 2006 there were 84 events in 15 different sporting areas.

WINTER OLYMPICS HOSTS
1924 Chamonix, France
1928 St Moritz, Switzerland
1932 Lake Placid, USA
1936 Garmisch-Partenkirchen, Germany
1948 St Moritz, Switzerland
1952 Oslo, Norway
1956 Cortina, Italy
1960 Squaw Valley, USA
1964 Innsbruck, Austria
1968 Grenoble, France
1972 Sapporo, Japan
1976 Innsbruck, Austria
1980 Lake Placid, USA
1984 Sarajevo, Yugoslavia (now Bosnia)
1988 Calgary, Canada
1992 Albertville, France
1994 Lillehammer, Norway
1998 Nagano, Japan
2002 Salt Lake City, USA
2006 Turin, Italy
2010 Vancouver, Canada

◄ An exciting moment from the ice-hockey match between France and the USA at the Lillehammer Winter Olympics in 1994. In the final, Sweden beat Canada to win gold.

SNOW JOKE

Far fewer countries send teams to the Winter Games than to the Summer. Poor countries with warm climates can rarely afford, for example, to construct ice rinks in which to train future champions. (But at Calgary in 1988, there was, believe it or not, a four-man bobsleigh team from Jamaica!) The mountainous countries of Europe have dominated the vast majority of the eighteen Games. Norway, the **USSR**, Sweden, Switzerland, and Germany have been especially successful in the final medals tables.

Often the Winter Olympians have to compete against the weather as well as one another. Rain, thaw, blizzard, and gale have all been problems – and in 1964 at Innsbruck, after a very mild winter, there was simply not enough snow for the Alpine skiing. Austrian troops had to transport more than 25,000 tonnes of the powdery stuff to the River Inn valley from higher snowfields!

One thing is for sure, the Olympics are never dull. What do you think will happen in future Olympic Games?

SPORTS FEATURED AT THE TURIN WINTER OLYMPICS, 2006	
Alpine skiing	Luge
Biathlon	Nordic combined
Bobsleigh	Short track speed skating
Cross-country skiing	Skeleton
Curling	Ski jumping
Figure skating	Snowboarding
Freestyle skiing	Speed skating
Ice hockey	

◀ Alpine skiing for both men and women is divided into five separate events: downhill, slalom, giant slalom, super-giant slalom, and Alpine combination (downhill and slalom). Here Luxembourg's Marc Girardelli is competing in the downhill at the Lillehammer Winter Olympics.

GLOSSARY

aggression warlike or hostile act

amateur someone who competes for fun, rather than as a job, and who is unpaid

apartheid policy of keeping black people apart from, and inferior to, whites

aristocrat a member of the upper or privileged classes

boycott to refuse to have anything to do with a person, country or event

Cold War period, after World War Two, of unfriendly relations between the USA and the USSR, which never quite became real warfare

Communism the idea that a single, ruling political party can provide for all its people better than if they are left to make their own decisions and keep their own homes, land, and businesses. The USSR became the first Communist state in 1917. After World War Two, the USSR introduced Communism into much of eastern Europe.

defect leave one country to live in another, without official permission

delegate someone sent to a meeting as a representative of another person or group of people

endorse to support something

equestrianism riding or performing on horseback

millennium period of 1,000 years. The current millennium started in 2000 and ends in 2999.

multicultural to do with people who come from different countries and have different ideas

national anthem song written to represent a country and celebrate national pride

Nazi short form of the National Socialist German Workers' Party, a political party led by Adolf Hitler

Parkinson's disease illness that affects a person's nerves

pentathlon athletic contest where a competitor takes part in five different events

professional paid competitor

public school (in Britain) school which charges fees from parents

reclaim make land useful or productive

royal box special seats from which the royal family views public events

sabre a curved sword

sponsorship the money given to pay for an event or support a person

track and field sporting events which involve running, jumping, throwing and walking – such as the 100 metres or the javelin

truce temporary halting of a war or fight

USSR a Communist country, including Russia and many smaller nations, which broke up in 1991

wreath an arrangement of leaves in the shape of a ring

FIND OUT MORE

USING THE INTERNET

Explore the Internet to find out more about the history of the Modern Olympic Games or to see pictures of the most recent Games. You can use a search engine such as www.yahooligans.com, or ask a question at www.ask.com. To find out more about the Modern Olympics, you could search by typing in key words such as Winter Olympics, Beijing 2008, Olympic bids, or Paralympics.

These are some useful websites to look at to find more information:

http://www.infoplease.com/spot/olympicstimeline.html
This website charts the history of the Olympics from ancient Greece to the present day.

http://www.topendsports.com/events/discontinued/list.htm
This website provides a full list of discontinued Olympic sports.

http://www.paralympic.org
Home of the IPC (International Paralympic Committee)

http://www.olympic.org
The official website of the Olympic Movement, with all the latest news and a countdown to the next Games.

BOOKS

Amazing Pace: The Story of Olympic Champion Michael Phelps from Sydney to Athens to Beijing, Paul McMullen (Rodale Books, 2006)

The Olympics: Athens to Athens 1896-2004, M. Jacques Rogge (Weidenfeld Nicolson Illustrated, 2004)

The Olympics: Facts, Figures and Fun, Liam McCann (Artists' and Photographers' Press Ltd, 2006)

INDEX